Contents

Grandma's White Bread

2 packages active dry yeast
2¼ cups lukewarm water
½ cup nonfat dry milk
2 tablespoons sugar
1 tablespoon salt
⅓ cup cooking oil
7 to 7½ cups sifted flour

Sprinkle yeast on lukewarm water; stir to dissolve. Add dry milk, sugar, salt, oil, and 3 cups flour. Beat with electric mixer at medium speed until smooth, about 3 minutes, scraping bowl occasionally. Or, beat with spoon until batter is smooth. Gradually add enough remaining flour to make a soft dough that leaves the sides of the bowl. Cover; let rest 15 minutes. Knead on floured surface until smooth and satiny, about 5 minutes. Divide dough in half; shape each half into a loaf. Place in two greased 9 x 5 x 3 inch loaf pans. Let rise until doubled, about 1 to 1½ hours. Bake in 400° oven 30 to 35 minutes or until loaves sound hollow when tapped. Remove from pans; cool on racks. Makes two loaves.

MORMONS SAY: WHEAT FOR MAN

Since February 27, 1833, Mormons have had special guidance as to what food is good for physical health. On that date Joseph Smith, the first prophet and president of The Church of Jesus Christ of Latter-day Saints, declared that he received a revelation from the Lord regarding food and drink. Among other things the revelation reads: "All grain is ordained for the use of man and of beasts, to be the staff of life . . . Nevertheless, wheat for man, and corn for the ox, and oats for the horse," etc. (Doctrine and Covenants, Section 89, Verses 14 and 17)

Butterflake Rolls

2 eggs
⅓ cup sugar
1 teaspoon salt
1¼ cups evaporated milk
6 to 8 cups flour
1 cup hot water
2 yeast cakes (or packages)
1 cup warm water (to be mixed with the yeast)

Dissolve the yeast in one cup warm water. Set aside. Beat eggs and add sugar, salt, canned milk, and the 1 cup hot water. Beating constantly, add yeast mixture. Add up to 5 cups flour gradually mixing well, turn out on a pastry cloth or bread board, knead until smooth and elastic, adding enough flour to make it workable—no more than necessary. Let rise. Roll out to ½ inch thick and spread with butter. Do this 5 times alternating shortening with butter. Cut with biscuit cutter and place in well greased muffin tins. Let rise 2 to 4 hours. Bake at 425° for 8 to 12 minutes. Yields 36 rolls.

Overnight Wheat Rolls

2 tablespoons yeast
⅓ cup warm water
1 cup milk, scalded
½ cup butter or margarine
½ cup sugar
3 eggs, beaten
1 teaspoon salt
5 cups flour, 2½ cup each of white and whole wheat

Add sugar, butter or margarine to milk. Let cool. Dissolve yeast in water and add to milk mixture. Add beaten eggs and stir in flour. Mixture must be sticky. Cover with foil and refrigerate overnight or 4 to 6 hours. Roll out on floured board ¾ inch thick and cut. Brush with egg mixture, beating 1 egg with 2 tablespoons water. Let rise 3 to 4 hours. Bake at 350° for 15 minutes. Yields 32 rolls.

Baking Powder Biscuits

2 cups flour, sifted
3 teaspoons baking powder
½ teaspoons salt
⅓ cup shortening or cooking oil
1 cup milk

Sift flour, baking powder, and salt together in mixing bowl. Add shortening and cut in with pastry blender or 2 knives until particles are size of rice grains. Add milk and stir until dough stiffens—dough should be rather soft. Turn dough onto floured board and knead from 12 to 15 times. Roll out ⅜ to ¾ inch thick. Cut with biscuit cutter dipped in flour. Place on greased baking pan. Bake 10 to 15 minutes at 450°, depending on thickness or until they are golden brown. Makes 12 to 15 medium biscuits.

Old Fashioned Whole Wheat Bread

1 packet yeast
⅓ cup lukewarm water
1 tablespoon melted shortening
1 tablespoon honey
1 tablespoon molasses
1 tablespoon salt
3 cups scalded milk
6 cups whole wheat flour

Soften yeast in water. Combine melted shortening, honey, molasses, salt and scalded milk. Cool to lukewarm and combine with yeast mixture. Add flour as needed. Shape into 2 loaves and place in greased loaf tins. Let rise to not quite double in bulk (1 to 2 hours). Bake at 350° for 1 hour and 10 minutes. Makes 2 medium sized loaves.

Raised Potato Doughnuts

1 cup sweet milk
½ cup shortening
½ cup sugar
½ cup white corn syrup
1 tablespoon salt
1 package yeast
¼ cup warm water
1 egg, beaten
½ cup mashed potatoes, moistened with
½ cup potato water
6 cups flour

Scald milk, add shortening, sugar, syrup and salt. When cool, add yeast softened in ¼ cup water and 1 teaspoon sugar. Add beaten egg and potatoes. Beat in flour until mixture is very stiff and leaves sides of bowl. Place in greased bowl and let rise until triple in bulk. Roll out ½ inch thick and cut with doughnut cutter. Let stand about an hour. Fry in hot oil. When doughnuts are cooled, dip in Orange Doughnut Glaze. (see below.) Yields 36 doughnuts.

Orange Doughnut Glaze

1 tablespoon butter
1 tablespoon lemon juice
1 tablespoon orange juice
1 teaspoon orange rind
1½ cups powdered sugar
pinch of salt
¼ cup warm water

Place butter, juice, rind, and water in bowl and heat over hot water until butter is melted. Remove and add sugar and salt; beat until smooth.

Brigham's Buttermilk Doughnuts

2 cups buttermilk
2 large eggs, beaten
1 cup sugar
3 tablespoons shortening
5 cups sifted flour
2 teaspoons soda
1 teaspoon baking powder
1 teaspoon salt
1 teaspoon grated nutmeg
¼ cup melted butter

Combine buttermilk, eggs, sugar, and blend well. Beat in sifted dry ingredients, then stir in melted butter. Roll or pat dough on floured board about ¼ inch thick and cut with 2½ inch doughnut cutter. Fry in hot fat (375°) until golden brown on both sides. Drain and sprinkle with sugar, if desired. Makes 2 dozen doughnuts.

Heavenly Scones

1 yeast cake
¼ cup warm water
1 egg
¼ cup sugar
¼ cup shortening
½ cup hot water
2½ cup flour
1 teaspoon salt

Dissolve yeast in ¼ cup warm water. Put sugar, salt, shortening in bowl. Add ½ cup hot water to dissolve. Beat the egg and add to mixture. When it cools, add yeast. Add flour, knead, and let rise for 1 hour. Knead down and roll out thinly and cut into strips. Use enough shortening in pan to cover strips of dough and fry just a few at a time. Lightly brown both sides. Serve with butter and honey. Makes 12 scones.

Cinnamon Rolls

2 cups scalded milk
½ cup lukewarm water
2 packages yeast
1 cup sugar
2 beaten eggs
½ cup chopped nuts
½ cup raisins
1 cup mashed potatoes or soak ½ cup instant
flakes—fill cup with boiling water
7 cups flour
½ cup shortening
1 teaspoon salt

Add yeast to water. Add shortening to scalded
milk. Add salt and sugar, then the potatoes and
eggs. Mix with electric mixer. Add yeast mixture.
Add 3 cups flour and beat, adding the rest of the
flour gradually. Do not knead. Stir in the raisins
and nuts (these can be put on top of the dough
after it is rolled out also). Cover and refrigerate
for 2 to 3 hours. When doubled, punch down
and divide into two portions. Roll each piece out,
spread with melted butter and sprinkle with cinnamon and sugar. Roll up and cut into 1 inch
slices. Place on buttered sheet. Let rise until doubled in size (about 1 hour). Bake at 325° for 20
to 25 minutes. Cool slightly and brush with
glaze. Makes about 2 dozen.
Cinnamon mixture—1 teaspoon cinnamon to ⅓
cup sugar for each half of dough.

Blueberry Muffins

½ cup butter
1 cup sugar
2 eggs
2 cups flour
1 teaspoon baking powder
1 teaspoon baking soda
¼ teaspoon salt
¼ teaspoon nutmeg
⅛ teaspoon cloves
¾ cup buttermilk
1 can blueberries, well drained

Cream butter and sugar until light and fluffy.
Add eggs, one at a time, beating well after each
addition. Sift together dry ingredients; add to
creamed mixture alternately with buttermilk. Stir
only until well mixed. Carefully fold in drained
blueberries. Do not stir. Fill paper-lined, 2 inch
muffin pan ⅔ full. Bake at 375° for about 20
minutes or until done. Makes 12 large muffins.

Crispy Apple Muffins

¼ cup shortening
½ cup sugar
1 egg
1½ cup flour
½ teaspoon salt
3 teaspoons baking powder
½ cup milk
1 cup chopped apples
½ cup brown sugar
½ teaspoon cinnamon
½ cup nuts

Cream shortening and sugar. Add egg and beat.
Add dry ingredients alternately with milk. Fold in
apples and place in greased tins. Sprinkle mixture
of brown sugar, nuts, and ½ teaspoon cinnamon
on top. Bake in 375° oven for 20 to 25 minutes.
Makes 20 muffins.

Banana Nut Bread

½ cup margarine
1 cup sugar
2 eggs
1 cup mashed bananas
¼ cup milk
1 teaspoon lemon juice
2 cups flour
1½ teaspoons baking powder
½ teaspoon baking soda
¼ teaspoon salt
½ cup chopped nuts

Cream margarine and sugar. Add eggs and beat. Add bananas, milk, and lemon juice. Sift dry ingredients, add nuts. Blend the two mixtures. Bake in well greased 8x4x3 inch loaf pan for 1 hour at 350°. Makes 1 loaf.

Raisin Bread

2 packets yeast dissolved in ¾ cup warm water,
2 cups milk
¼ cup butter or margarine
1 teaspoon salt
½ cup sugar
2 eggs
about 5½ cups flour
1 cup raisins

Sprinkle yeast and 2 teaspoons sugar over warm water and set aside. Scald milk, add butter, salt, and sugar. When cooled, stir in yeast, beaten eggs, 2 cups flour and raisins. Beat well. Stir in enough flour for soft dough. Knead 5 minutes, let rise 1½ times bulk. Punch down, set 10 minutes. Shape in loaves. Let rise and bake 375° for 45 minutes. Glaze with powdered sugar icing. Makes 2 loaves.

Corn Bread

1 cup flour
1 cup yellow cornmeal
3½ teaspoons baking powder
1 teaspoon salt
3 tablespoons sugar
1 egg, slightly beaten
1 cup milk
¼ cup cooking oil

Sift together flour, cornmeal, baking powder, salt and sugar. Add remaining ingredients. Stir until flour is moistened, do not beat. Pour into greased 8 x 8 inch pan. Bake at 425° for 20 to 25 minutes.

Apricot Bread

1 cup dried apricots
1 cup warm water
1 cup sugar
2 tablespoons butter, melted
¼ cup reserved juice or apricot nectar
½ cup orange juice concentrate
2 cups flour
2 teaspoons baking powder
¼ teaspoon soda
1 cup chopped nuts

Chop apricots; soak 30 minutes in water; drain and save excess water (if there is none, use apricot nectar). Stir in sugar, butter, ¼ cup reserved juice, and orange juice concentrate. Sift together flour, baking powder, and soda; add nuts coated with flour mixture. Combine all ingredients; stir only enough to mix well; let stand 20 minutes before cooking. Grease and flour a loaf pan; bake for 1 hour and 15 minutes at 325°. Makes one loaf. Good with cream cheese.

Zucchini Loaf

1 cup sugar
1 cup brown sugar
3 eggs
1 cup salad oil
3 teaspoons vanilla
2 cups grated zucchini (if large, remove seeds)
1 cup raisins
½ cup nuts
Sift together:
3 cups flour
1 teaspoon soda
1 teaspoon salt
3 teaspoons cinnamon
¼ teaspoon baking powder

Combine wet and dry ingredients. Mix well. Put into greased and floured pans. Bake 1 hour at 325°. Makes 2 loaves.

Buttermilk Pancakes

2 cups flour
2 tablespoons sugar
1 teaspoon salt
1 teaspoon soda
2 cups buttermilk
2 tablespoons butter

Stir together and cook on pancake griddle.

Wheat Cakes

1⅓ cups sifted whole wheat flour
3 teaspoons baking powder
3 tablespoons sugar
¾ teaspoon salt
3 eggs, well beaten
1¼ cups milk
3 tablespoons bacon drippings or melted
shortening

Stir together dry ingredients. Combine eggs and milk, then stir into dry ingredients along with drippings, mixing only until blended. For lighter pancakes, eggs may be separated and stiffly beaten egg whites folded into batter just before baking. Bake on lightly greased griddle until golden brown, then turn. Makes twelve 4 inch pancakes. This batter makes good waffles too.

Chokecherry Syrup

1 pint (2 cups) chokecherry juice
3 cups sugar
½ cup light corn syrup

Chokecherry juice is made by boiling chokecherries in just enough water to cover until berries are mushy. Strain the juice through cheesecloth. Simmer all ingredients together, uncovered, over moderately low heat in a large heavy enamel or stainless-steel saucepan about 15 minutes or until mixture is thick and syrupy. Pour into a heatproof pitcher and serve on pancakes in place of maple syrup. Makes about 1 pint.

Sourdough Pancakes

1 cup sourdough starter (see below)
1 cup flour
2¼ teaspoons baking powder
¼ teaspoon baking soda
¼ teaspoon salt
1 egg
2 tablespoons oil
½ to ¾ cup milk (depending on thickness desired)

Mix all ingredients. Using a scant ¼ cup batter per pancake, bake on a hot, greased griddle about 3 minutes, or until the tops are bubbly and edges are brown, then turn. Makes about 10 pancakes.

Sourdough Starter

2 cups flour
3 tablespoons sugar
1 envelope active dry yeast
1 teaspoon salt
2 cups warm water 105° to 115°

In large bowl mix all dry ingredients. Gradually stir in water, whisk until smooth. Cover with a towel and set in a warm (80° to 85°) draft-free place. Stir 2 to 3 times a day for three days or until bubbly. Transfer to larger bowl. Cover partially (tilt lid or punch holes in plastic cover) and refrigerate.
Replenish Starter after each use. If longer than 14 days, put it in the freezer until it is needed. To replenish after using, whisk in 1 cup flour, 1 cup milk, and ½ cup sugar. DON'T USE FOR AT LEAST 24 HOURS.

Buttermilk Pancakes

Hearty Vegetable Soup

3 pounds beef shank cross cuts
8 cups water
4 teaspoons salt
½ teaspoon dried oregano, crushed
¼ teaspoon dried marjoram, crushed
5 whole black peppercorns
2 bay leaves
1 16 ounce can tomatoes, cut up
1 15½ ounce can red kidney beans
2 cups frozen, whole, small onions or 3 medium onions, quartered
1 medium potato, peeled and diced
1 cup sliced celery
1 cup sliced carrots

In large saucepan or Dutch oven place beef, water, salt, oregano, marjoram, peppercorns, and bay leaves. Bring to boil; reduce heat, cover and simmer, 2 hours. Remove beef; cut meat from bones in large cubes. Strain broth; skim off excess fat. Return broth to saucepan; add meat, undrained tomatoes, beans, onions, potatoes, celery, and carrots. Simmer, covered, 1 hour. Season to taste with salt and pepper. Serves 10 to 12.

Creamy Chicken Noodle Soup

8 cups chicken broth or bouillon
1 to 2 cups diced cooked chicken
1 cup milk
1 cup quartered, thinly sliced carrots
1 cup sliced celery, including some leaves
½ cup chopped green pepper
½ cup chopped onion
1 clove garlic, minced
½ teaspoon dried marjoram leaves, crushed
salt
freshly ground pepper

In a large kettle combine broth or bouillon, chicken, milk, carrot, celery, green pepper, onion, garlic, marjoram and salt and pepper. Cook over medium heat until vegetables are crisp and tender.

6 ounces homemade noodles (recipe below)
½ cup milk
¼ cup all-purpose flour
2 tablespoons butter or margarine

Add noodles and cook until almost done. In a cup, whisk together milk and flour; stir into soup mixture and boil gently for 3 minutes. Stir in butter or margarine. Makes 8 to 10 servings.

Homemade Noodles

1 teaspoon salt
2 cups all-purpose flour
3 eggs
1 tablespoon vegetable oil
2 to 4 tablespoons cold water

Place flour and salt in a large bowl; make a depression in the center and add eggs and oil. Gradually stir in flour from the edges adding water, 1 tablespoon at a time, until flour is moistened enough to form a ball. Divide dough into 4 equal parts. Roll one part at a time into paper-thin rectangle on well-floured board. Loosely fold lengthwise into thirds and cut crosswise into strips. Narrow noodles about ⅛ inch strips; wide ones about ¼ inch strips on towel until stiff and dry, about 2 hours. Break dry strips into smaller pieces. Cook in boiling salted water until noodles are tender. Serves 8 to 10.

Cream of Zucchini Soup

1 medium onion, chopped
2 tablespoons butter or margarine
2 cups (2 medium) zucchini squash
2 cups chicken broth
1/8 teaspoon freshly ground black pepper
1/8 teaspoon nutmeg
1/8 teaspoon salt
1/2 cup half-and-half
Cheddar cheese, shredded

Clean, chop and cook onion in butter until soft and transparent but not browned. Wash and slice zucchini. Combine onion, zucchini and chicken broth in large saucepan. Bring to boil; simmer 15 minutes or until squash is tender. Add seasonings. Puree mixture in blender or food processor until smooth; return to saucepan. Add half-and-half cream; adjust seasonings to taste. Reheat but do not boil. Serve hot, garnished with shredded Cheddar cheese. 4 servings.

Potato-Cheese Soup

2 potatoes, peeled and cut into cubes (2 cups)
2 cups water
1/2 cup chopped carrot
1/2 cup chopped celery
1/2 cup chopped onion
2 teaspoons chicken bouillon granules
1/4 cup butter
1/4 flour
1 pint half and half
1/8 teaspoon freshly ground pepper.
2 ounces Swiss cheese, shredded
2 ounces sharp Cheddar cheese, shredded

Cook vegetables in water and bouillon until tender. Melt butter in pan, add flour. Add half and half to thicken. Stir in the cheese until melted, and add to cooked vegetables. Do not boil. Serve hot for 8 servings.

Navy Bean Soup

1 pound dry navy beans
1 meaty ham bone or 1 1/2 pounds ham hocks
1 cup chopped onion
2 garlic cloves, minced
1 cup chopped celery
2/3 cup mashed potato
1/4 cup chopped parsley
1 1/2 teaspoons salt
1/2 teaspoon pepper
1 teaspoon nutmeg
1 teaspoon oregano
1 teaspoon basil
1 bay leaf

In large kettle, cover beans with 6 to 8 cups water. Bring to a boil and cook 2 minutes. Remove from heat and cover; let stand one hour. Drain; add 2 quarts water and ham bone. Bring to boil again and simmer about 1 1/2 hours, until beans are tender. Add remaining ingredients and simmer another 20 to 30 minutes. Makes 3 quarts, about 10 to 12 servings.

Split Pea Soup

1 pound split peas
1/4 pound bacon, diced
2 medium onions, thinly sliced
2 carrots, thinly sliced
1 cup celery, sliced
2 bay leaves
3 teaspoons salt
1/4 teaspoon thyme
1/4 teaspoon black pepper
2 quarts water
1 large potato, grated raw
meaty ham bone, if available

Soak split peas 3 hours or overnight. In large soup kettle, saute bacon pieces, onions, carrots, until onions are golden. Add split peas after rinsing and draining. Add celery, bay leaves, seasonings and 2 quarts water. Grate large, peeled potato, into mixture; add meaty ham bone, cover, simmer 3 to 4 hours. Discard bay leaves. Cut meat from ham bone and return meat to soup mixture. Serves 6 generously.

❧ Salads & Sauces ❧

Savory Potato Salad

Savory Potato Salad

4 cups cooked, peeled russet potatoes
1 cup coarsely chopped celery
½ cup grated onion
5 hard-cooked eggs, coarsely chopped
½ cup chopped sweet pickles
2 tablespoons chopped pimiento
1 teaspoon seasoning salt
1½ teaspoons celery seeds (optional)
freshly ground pepper
¾ to 1 cup real mayonnaise
1 teaspoon prepared mustard

In a large bowl combine cubed potatoes, celery, onion, eggs, pickles, pimiento, salt, optional celery seeds and pepper. In small bowl combine mayonnaise and mustard. Gently stir into potato mixture. Serves 8.

Mixed Bean Salad

1 can (#2 size) of each:
French-cut green beans
cut green beans
yellow wax beans
red kidney beans
Dressing:

½ cup sugar	½ cup salad oil
1 tablespoon salt	½ cup diced white onion
½ teaspoon pepper	½ cup vinegar

Drain liquid from each can, rinse contents in cold water and drain. Mix all ingredients for dressing, pour over beans. Let set 48 hours for best results. Keep covered and in the refrigerator. Add a few onion rings for garnish.

Mom's Cole Slaw

1 tablespoon sugar
1 teaspoon dry mustard
¼ teaspoon salt
few grains of pepper
2 tablespoons melted butter or margarine
1 egg beaten
¾ cup light cream
¼ cup vinegar
4 cups shredded cabbage
paprika

Combine sugar, mustard, salt, pepper, and egg. Add melted butter and cream; mix well. Add vinegar very slowly; cook over hot water, stirring constantly until mixture thickens. Chill. Toss dressing with shredded cabbage; sprinkle with paprika. Makes 6 servings.

Curry Chicken Salad

2 cups cooked chicken, cut into large cubes
1 teaspoon curry powder
2 cups celery, cut on the slant
1 cup mayonnaise
1 small green pepper, cut fine
A shake or two of pepper

Combine all the ingredients and chill. The salad may be garnished with green seedless grapes. Serves about 6.

Zesty Barbecue Sauce

1 onion, chopped
1⅓ tablespoon salt
2 tablespoons fat
½ green pepper
1 cup chopped celery
1 teaspoon chili powder
2 tablespoons vinegar
2 tablespoons brown sugar
dash of cinnamon or nutmeg

Cook green peppers, onions and celery until tender. Add the rest of the ingredients and simmer 30 minutes.

Add the following:
4 tablespoons lemon juice
½ teaspoon prepared mustard
2 tablespoons Worcestershire sauce
1½ cups tomato juice
1½ cups tomato catsup

Simmer 10 more minutes. Makes 2 cups.

Mormon Gravy

Mormon gravy was common fare among the early settlers. It is still hearty and nourishing for many of their descendants who like to make it with ground beef or frizzled bacon or ham, and serve it over baked potatoes. The pioneers often spooned it generously over meat pies, made from small pieces of leftover meat or poultry cooked together with such vegetables as carrots, potatoes, turnips, onions, and seasoned with salt and pepper.

4 tablespoons meat drippings (bacon, beef, or ham)
3 tablespoons flour
2 cups milk
salt
pepper
paprika

Remove any meat from pan and measure fat. Return desired amount of fat to skillet. Add flour and brown slightly if desired. Remove from heat and add milk, stirring well to blend. Return to heat and cook and stir until mixture is thick and smooth. Season to taste. Serves 6 to 8. Serve with potatoes, biscuits, corn bread, or even pancakes or waffles.

Hollandaise Sauce

2 egg yolks
Salt, cayenne pepper to taste
1 to 2 tablespoons lemon juice
½ cup melted butter
whipping cream

Place egg yolks, lemon juice, salt, and cayenne in blender container. Cover. Blend on low speed 5 seconds. Remove cap. Pour in butter in a slow, steady stream. Continue blending only until sauce has thickened. Should it curdle, add additional egg yolks. Blend at high speed while adding whipping cream 1 tablespoon at a time until sauce reconstitutes. Makes about 1 cup. Use immediately.

Chantilly Sauce

½ cup whipping cream
1 cup Hollandaise Sauce

Whip cream until stiff. Gently fold in the Hollandaise. Makes 2 cups.

Homemade Red Chili Sauce

6 ounces whole dried ancho-pasilla or California chilies (or combination)
3 cups hot water
¼ cup tomato sauce or tomato paste
1 small clove garlic, minced
¼ cup salad oil
1½ teaspoons salt
1 teaspoon oregano
¼ teaspoon ground cumin

Mix well and cook over a medium heat until blended.

Citrus Fruit Dip

1 egg, beaten
½ cup sugar
1 tablespoon orange peel
1 teaspoon lemon peel
2 tablespoons fresh lemon juice
1 cup whipped cream

Beat egg and sugar together. Add orange peel, lemon peel and lemon juice. Cook over low heat until thick. Cool the mixture then fold in whipped cream.

Hearty Turkey Pie

2 cups diced cooked turkey
1½ cups cooked vegetables (peas, carrots or green beans)
1 cup diced cooked potatoes
¼ cup butter or margarine
⅓ cup flour
½ teaspoon salt
½ teaspoon ground poultry seasonings or sage
3 cups milk
1 9 inch two-crust pastry

Combine turkey and vegetables in a dish. Melt butter in saucepan. Blend in flour, salt and seasonings. Remove from heat. Add milk gradually. Stir and cook until mixture thickens. Add a little more milk if too thick. Combine with turkey and vegetables. Pour into pastry shell. Cover with top crust. Seal and flute edges. Slit top in several places. Bake at 425° for 35 to 40 minutes (until golden brown). Yield 6 servings.

Barbecue Chicken

1 large chicken, cut into serving pieces
¾ cup chopped onion
½ cup cooking oil
¾ cup tomato catsup
¾ cup water
¼ cup lemon juice
3 tablespoons sugar
3 tablespoons Worcestershire sauce
2 tablespoons prepared mustard
2 teaspoons salt
½ teaspoon pepper

Cook onion in a little water until soft. Mix the remaining ingredients and heat. Pour into the onions and simmer for 15 minutes. Line a 13 x 9 inch cake pan with foil (for easy clean up). Arrange the chicken pieces in pan and pour the sauce over it. Bake 1½ to 2 hours at 350°. Place the cover on the dish, or cover with foil if using cake pan, after sauce has started to bubble. Serves 6. Also good for hamburgers and hot dogs.

Chicken and Dumplings

1 5 to 6 pound stewing chicken, cut up, or 2 to 3 pound broiler-fryer chicken
4 stalks celery with leaves, cut up
2 carrots, cut up
1 small onion, sliced
1 sprig parsley, cut up
1 bay leaf
2 teaspoons salt
¼ teaspoon pepper

Homemade dumplings:
1 cup all-purpose flour
2 teaspoons baking powder
½ teaspoon salt
½ cup milk
2 tablespoons cooking oil
2 tablespoons snipped parsley

In Dutch oven or large kettle, cover raw chicken with water. Add celery and next 6 ingredients. Place lid on kettle, bring to boiling point and reduce heat. Simmer until meat is tender (about 2½ hours). Remove kettle from stove. With slotted spoon or tongs, remove chicken pieces to shallow container. Allow to cool slightly. Remove skin and bones from chicken and set chicken pieces aside. Strain soup into clean container, discarding all vegetable and scum material. Return soup to stove and bring to a boil. Prepare homemade dumplings by combining flour, baking powder, and salt. Add milk, cooking oil, and parsley. Stir to moisten.
To the boiling broth, add chicken pieces first, then dumplings (by dropping them from tablespoon) directly into boiling stock. Cover tightly; bring to boil again. Do not remove cover, but watch kettle carefully and reduce heat before it boils over. Simmer 12 to 15 minutes to cook dumplings. Remove chicken and dumplings to platter and keep hot.
Turn heat to high, and allow broth to boil again. Make a white sauce by combining 1 cup cold water with 4 tablespoons flour. Beat until smooth. Stir into boiling broth and cook until thick and broth is clear. Season with salt and pepper to taste. Pour over chicken and dumplings. Serve hot. Makes 6 to 8 servings.

Home Style Bread Dressing

½ cup butter
¾ cup celery, diced
¾ cup onions, chopped
6 cups dried bread cut into cubes
3 eggs, beaten
1 teaspoon salt
1 teaspoon pepper
½ teaspoon poultry seasoning
1⅓ tablespoon parsley
½ teaspoon sage
½ cup bouillon

Cook onion and celery in butter. In a large bowl, combine all ingredients adding water as necessary. Season to taste. Loosely pack mixture into cavity of turkey or roasting chicken.
To serve as a side dish, put mixture into a covered casserole and bake at 325° for half an hour. Serves 8.

Roast Wild Duck

6 ducks—Mallard or Teal
6 strips bacon
5 tablespoons flour with salt and pepper
2 cups water

Chop for stuffing:
1 onion
1 bell pepper
1 apple
1 lemon
2 tablespoons olive oil

Chop for gravy:
2 onions
2 bell peppers
1 stalk celery

Mix stuffing ingredients with olive oil. Wash ducks well, season with salt and pepper and fill cavities with stuffing. Sprinkle ducks with flour. Fry bacon, reserve drippings. Brown ducks in bacon drippings in a black iron pot. Remove ducks and pour off excess fat. Return ducks to pot, add chopped ingredients for gravy, add water and cover. Roast in 350° oven until ducks begin to break at breastbone. Add additional water if necessary to keep ducks moist. Place on serving platter and garnish with crab apple and parsley. Serve with gravy over rice and potatoes if desired. Serves 6.

Leg of Lamb

1 leg of lamb
salt
pepper
¼ cup vinegar
¼ cup Worcestershire sauce
brown sugar
2 garlic cloves

Wipe lamb with damp cloth. Rub lamb with salt and pepper. Put in an open pan with no water. Mix vinegar and Worcestershire sauce and pour over lamb. Cover roast with brown sugar. Slice garlic buds very thin and put on top. Place in cold oven. Heat to 325°, cook 30 minutes per pound. Serves 6 to 8.

Lamb Vegetable Supper

1 pound boneless lamb, cut in 1 inch cubes
2 tablespoons all-purpose flour
3 tablespoons cooking oil
1 clove garlic, minced
1 bay leaf
½ teaspoon dried basil, crushed
¼ teaspoon dried thyme, crushed
2½ cups water
1½ teaspoons salt
⅛ teaspoon pepper
4 medium potatoes, peeled and quartered
3 carrots, cut in ¾ inch pieces
2 onions, cut in eighths
1 tomato

Coat lamb with flour. In heavy 3 quart saucepan brown the lamb, half at a time, in hot oil. Drain. Add garlic, bay leaf, basil, thyme, water, salt, and pepper. Simmer, covered, 30 minutes. Add potatoes, carrots, and onions; simmer, covered, until vegetables are tender, about 20 minutes. Peel tomato; cut into 6 wedges. Add to stew; cook, covered, to heat through (2 to 3 minutes). Remove bay leaf. Serves 4.

Bacon-draped Roast Venison

1 loin or saddle of venison, 5 to 6 pounds
1 teaspoon salt
¼ teaspoon freshly ground pepper
¼ teaspoon crumbled leaf rosemary (optional)
½ pound sliced bacon

Rub the roast well with salt and pepper and, if you like, the rosemary. Stand in a shallow roasting pan, resting roast on its rib end. Drape bacon slices over the roast, covering it completely. Insert a meat thermometer into the meat, not touching bone. Roast uncovered in a moderate oven at 350°, allowing 15 to 20 minutes per pound for rare meat (125° to 130° on the meat thermometer) and 25 minutes per pound for medium (140° on the meat thermometer.)

Venison Swiss Steak

1½ pounds venison steak (1½ inch thick)
3 large onions, sliced
6 ribs celery, cut in thirds
2 cups canned tomatoes
2 tablespoons Worcestershire sauce
salt and pepper
1 to 2 tablespoons flour dissolved in ¼ cup cold water.

Dust venison steak with flour, salt and pepper. Brown in hot fat. Mix other ingredients, except flour and spread over meat. Cook, covered, over low heat, 1¼ to 1½ hours. Remove meat and thicken juice by adding flour mixed with cold water. Serves 4 to 6.

Pork Chops'n Stuffing

4 to 6 pork chops
3 cups soft bread crumbs
2 tablespoons chopped onion
¼ to ½ teaspoon poultry seasoning
1 can cream of mushroom soup
½ cup water
A little chopped celery (optional)

Brown chops on both sides; place in shallow baking dish. Mix bread cubes, onion, chopped celery and poultry seasoning. In a separate bowl mix soup and water together and fold into bread mixture. Place mounds of stuffing on each chop. Bake at 350° for 1 hour. Serves 4 to 5.

Tangy Mustard Rainbow Trout

6 pan-dressed rainbow trout or other small fish,
fresh or frozen
¾ teaspoon salt
3 tablespoons butter or margarine, melted
¾ cup prepared mustard
¾ cup sugar
¾ cup water
¾ cup vinegar
⅛ teaspoon liquid red pepper sauce
4 teaspoons cornstarch
¼ teaspoon salt
2 chicken bouillon cubes (optional)
6 servings hot, fluffy rice

Thaw frozen fish. Wash and pat dry. Arrange fish
in well-greased, shallow baking pan. Sprinkle
inside and out with salt. Drizzle butter or
margarine over fish. Bake in moderate oven, 350°,
25 to 30 minutes or until fish flakes easily when
tested with a fork. While fish is baking, prepare
sauce. Combine remaining ingredients, except
rice, in heavy saucepan in order listed; beat until
well mixed. Cook over medium heat, stirring
constantly, until thickened. Serve over trout and
rice. Makes 6 servings.

Baked Stuffed Fish

1 tablespoon flour
2 onions sliced and separated into rings
3 to 4 pound fish, dressed for stuffing
salt and pepper
1 package (5 ounces) seasoned stuffing mix
¼ cup butter or margarine, melted
1 tablespoon lemon juice

Shake flour in family size (14 x 20 inch) brown-
in-bag; place in 2 inch deep roasting pan, large
enough to allow fish to lie flat. Place onion rings
in bottom of bag. Rinse fish and wipe dry. Cut
fish inside along each side of backbone and
remove bone but leave skin uncut. Sprinkle inside
and out with salt and pepper. Prepare stuffing
mix by package directions. Stuff fish with
mixture. Close stuffed area with toothpicks. Place
prepared fish on onion rings in bag. Spoon on
melted butter or margarine and lemon juice.
Close bag with twist tie; make six half inch slits
in top of bag. Bake for 40 minutes or until fish
flakes easily when tested with a fork through bag.
Bake at 350°. Makes 6 to 8 servings. <u>NOTE:</u>
Fish may be garnished by cutting slits across top
of baked fish at 2 inch intervals or where serving
cuts will be made and inserting lemon wedges. Or
top fish with lightly cooked bacon strips.

Venison Swiss Steak

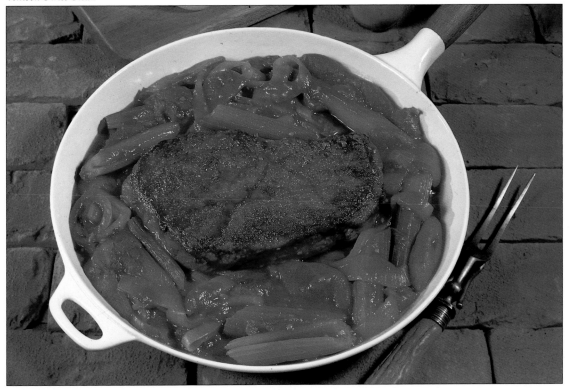

Dad's Barbecued Spareribs

3 pounds farm style spareribs
2 tablespoons vinegar
1 tablespoon butter
5 tablespoons lemon juice
4 tablespoons Worcestershire sauce
1 cup water
salt and pepper
2 onions
2 tablespoons brown sugar
1 small bottle catsup
1 tablespoon prepared mustard
2 tablespoons paprika

Boil all ingredients for 20 minutes or pressure cook for 5 minutes. Pour over spareribs. Bake 1 hour at 375°. Serves 8.

Easy Meat Loaf

2 pounds ground beef
2 eggs
1½ cups bread crumbs
1 package onion soup mix
½ cup warm water
¾ cup catsup
8 ounces tomato sauce
3 slices bacon

Stir meat, eggs, bread crumbs, onion soup mix, water, and catsup together. Put in loaf pan. Put bacon strips on meat mixture. Pour tomato sauce over top. Bake at 350° for 1 hour. Serves 8.

Country Beef Pie

The Crust:
½ cup canned tomato sauce
1 pound ground beef
¼ cup chopped green pepper
⅛ teaspoon oregano
½ cup bread crumbs
¼ cup chopped onion
1½ teaspoons salt
⅛ teaspoon pepper

The Filling:
1⅓ cup minute rice
1½ cup canned tomato sauce
½ cup grated cheddar cheese
1 cup water
½ teaspoon salt

Combine ingredients for crust and mix well. Pat into bottom of 9 inch pie tin. Pinch 1 inch flutings around edges.
Combine ingredients for filling except for cheese. Spoon rice mixture into meat shell. Cover with foil. Bake at 350° for 45 minutes. Uncover and sprinkle top with cheese. Return to oven and bake uncovered 10 to 15 minutes longer. Cut into pie-shaped pieces. Makes 5 or 6 servings.

Savory Swiss Steak

1½ pound round steak
¼ cup flour
¾ teaspoon salt
2 tablespoons oil
1 small onion, diced
1 small green pepper, diced
2½ cups canned tomatoes

Have steak cut two inches thick. Mix salt and flour, chop or pound into meat on both sides. Brown the steak on both sides in hot fat. Add onions and green peppers, cook until tender. Add tomatoes and cover tightly and simmer for 2 hours or until meat is tender, or bake in oven at 300° for 3 hours, using a heavy pan with a tight-fitting lid. Makes 6 servings.

"Yea, flesh of the beasts and of the fowls have been ordained for the use of man with thanksgiving; nevertheless they are to be used sparingly." (Doctrine and Covenants, Section 89, Verse 12). The Word of Wisdom counsels that man should do all things in moderation. Mormons believe that meat is an essential part of the diet, but it must be used sparingly to be truly beneficial to man's health.

Pot Roast with Vegetables

3 pounds beef pot roast coated with flour
¼ cup fat
2 teaspoons salt
¼ teaspoon pepper
1 cup water
6 potatoes, cut in half
6 medium peeled carrots
6 medium peeled onions
6 small peeled turnips
¼ cup flour

Brown pot roast in hot fat. Add salt, pepper and water. Cover and cook slowly for 2 hours. Add more water if necessary to prevent burning. When meat is nearly tender, add vegetables and cook ½ hour or until vegetables are tender. Remove meat and vegetables to a platter and make gravy by adding water to kettle to make 2 cups broth. Mix the ¼ cup flour with ½ cup cold water. Stir and add slowly to the broth. Boil 5 minutes, season to taste. Serves 6 to 8.

Hamburger Stroganoff

1½ pounds ground beef
2 tablespoons butter
2 tablespoons salad oil
1 cup chopped onion
6 ounce can mushrooms
1 can beef bouillon soup
1½ tablespoons flour
dash of nutmeg
dash of Worcestershire sauce
salt and pepper to taste
2 cups sour cream

Place hamburger in large, heavy skillet and brown thoroughly. Remove skillet from heat. Pour contents of skillet into strainer to drain and discard fat. Melt butter and oil in skillet, and saute onion and mushrooms until onions are clear. Remove from skillet and set aside. Add flour to oil mixture in skillet and brown over medium heat. Add bouillon and blend. Stir in salt, pepper, and nutmeg. Return meat, onions, and mushrooms to skillet. Simmer all together for 15 minutes. Just before serving, stir in sour cream. Serve over noodles. Makes 6 to 8 servings.

Spicy Chili

3 cups pinto beans
1 quart bottle tomatoes, or 2 to 1 pound cans
2 pounds ground beef
2 medium onions, chopped
1 to 2 chopped green peppers
2 cloves garlic, crushed or chopped (more if desired)
2 to 3 tablespoons chili powder
1 teaspoon pepper
1 tablespoon cumin
1 teaspoon salt

Parboil dry beans until soft (about 1 to 2 hours). Drain well. Put all ingredients in crock pot in order listed. Stir once. Cover and cook on low 10 hours or longer. Serves 12.

Old Fashioned Beef Stew

2 pounds beef stew, cut into 1½ inches cubes
2 teaspoons salt
½ cup flour
1 teaspoon sugar
2 tablespoons oil
6 carrots, peeled and sliced or quartered
1 bay leaf
1 cup sliced celery
1 tablespoon Worcestershire sauce
4 potatoes, peeled and cut into eighths
1 onion, chopped
12 small white onions
1 cup beef bouillon
¼ teaspoon pepper
4 cups water

Coat meat with flour; set excess flour aside. In large skillet or slow cooking pot, with browning unit, heat oil. Brown meat on all sides. In slow-cooking pot, combine browned beef, bay leaf, Worcestershire sauce, chopped onion, bouillon, pepper, salt, sugar, and vegetables. Pour water over all. Cover and cook on low 8 to 10 hours. Turn control on high. Thicken with flour left over from coating (about ¼ cup) dissolved in a small amount of water. Cover and cook on high 10 to 15 minutes or until slightly thickened. Makes 6 to 8 servings.

Mama's Lasagna

½ pound lasagna noodles
2 tablespoons vegetable oil
2 cloves minced garlic
1 medium onion, chopped
1 pound ground beef
1 teaspoon salt
¼ teaspoon pepper
1 can (2 pounds 3 ounces) tomato sauce
Italian tomatoes, crushed
2 cans (6 ounces) tomato paste
½ teaspoon dried basil
1 teaspoon dried oregano leaves
1 teaspoon sugar
1 pound ricotta cheese
1 jar (3 ounces) parmesan cheese
2 beaten eggs
1 pound mozzarella cheese
1 tablespoon minced parsley

Heat vegetable oil in skillet. Cook garlic and onions until soft. Add beef and seasoning and cook until crumbly. Add tomato sauce, paste, tomatoes, and spices. Simmer one hour. Cook noodles in salted water about 15 minutes. Drain, rinse and set aside. Blend beaten eggs, ricotta, mozzarella, and parsley in a bowl. In a baking dish 9 x 13 x 2 inch, layer meat sauce, noodles, and cheese mixture, ending with noodles. Top with mozzarella and parmesan cheese. Bake at 350° for 30 to 45 minutes. Let stand 10 minutes. Makes 12 servings.

Baked Noodle Casserole

1½ pound ground beef
1 green pepper, chopped
2 small onions, chopped
1 cup celery, chopped
1 (4 ounces) can mushrooms
1 can tomato soup
1 large can tomatoes
1 pound package of narrow egg noodles
1 teaspoon chili powder
1 cup grated cheese
salt and pepper to taste

Cook noodles until tender in boiling salted water, about 10 minutes. Drain, rinse, and set aside. Brown beef, add celery, onions, green pepper, salt, and pepper and cook 10 minutes. Add the remainder of the ingredients, including cooked noodles. Put in casserole dish and place grated cheese on top. Bake about one hour at 325°. Serves 8 to 10.

Delicious Beef and Rice

1 pound ground beef
1 cup rice
1 small onion, chopped
2 tablespoons oil
1 teaspoon each salt, paprika
½ teaspoon pepper
1 small bottle of olives, sliced
2 cups tomato juice
½ cup grated cheese

Brown ground beef with rice and onion in oil in skillet, stirring until crumbly. Add remaining ingredients (except cheese) with 1½ cups boiling water. Bake covered at 300° for 1 hour. Top with cheese. Bake uncovered, for 10 minutes longer or until cheese is melted. Yields 6 servings.

Bean Casserole

1 large can pork and beans
1 small can lima beans drained
1 can kidney beans
1 large onion, chopped
½ cup brown sugar
½ pound ground beef
½ cup catsup
1 tablespoon dry mustard
6 strips bacon

Brown meat and onions in large skillet over high heat. Mix remaining ingredients and mix well. Put into casserole dish. Cut bacon strips in half and lay on top of casserole. Bake at 350° for 3 to 4 hours uncovered. Serves 8 to 10.

Turkey or Chicken Casserole

¼ cup chopped onion
¼ cup chopped celery
½ cube margarine
6 cups soft bread crumbs
1 can boned turkey or chicken
1 teaspoon sage
¼ teaspoon salt
⅛ teaspoon pepper
1 can cream of chicken soup
½ soup can of milk

Fry onion and celery in margarine until clear. Add bread crumbs, turkey, sage, salt and pepper to make dressing. Blend soup and milk together. In casserole dish, layer dressing, then soup mixture. Sprinkle a few bread crumbs on top. Bake 350° for 30 minutes. Yields 6 to 8 servings.

Hamburger Casserole

1 pound ground beef
1 small onion, grated
1 teaspoon salt
½ teaspoon sugar
¼ teaspoon pepper
1 cup grated carrots
1 cup grated potatoes
1 beaten egg
1 can mushroom soup
1 small can evaporated milk

In a skillet brown ground beef and onion. Place carrots, potatoes, and beef in a 1½ quart casserole dish. Mix the remaining ingredients, pour over casserole. Bake uncovered, at 325° for 40 minutes. Serves 6.

Cheesy Potato Casserole

6 to 7 boiled potatoes
1 pint sour cream
1 can cream of chicken soup, diluted with ¼
cup water
1 cup shredded cheese
1 tablespoon chopped onions or chives
¼ cup melted butter
salt and pepper to taste
corn flakes

Wash and boil potatoes (leave at a stage you can
grate) Cool and peel. Grate on coarse part of
grater. Place in buttered dripper pan. Mix
together sour cream, chicken soup and water, ½
cup cheese, onion or chives, salt and pepper. Put
on top of potatoes. Top with crushed corn flakes
and melted butter. Sprinkle on the other ½ cup
cheese. Bake at 350° for 30 minutes. Serves 10
to 14.

Ham & Potato Casserole

8 medium potatoes, peeled and cubed
3 cups cubed, fully cooked ham
¼ cup finely chopped onion
2 tablespoons snipped parsley
1 11 ounce can Cheddar cheese soup
1 10½ ounce can cream of celery soup
¾ cup milk
1 9 ounce package frozen cut green beans, thawed
1 cup soft bread crumbs (1½ slices bread)
2 tablespoons butter or margarine, melted

In greased 13 x 9 x 2 inch baking dish layer half of
the potatoes and half of the ham; sprinkle with
onion and parsley. Top with remaining potatoes
and ham. Mix soups, milk and ¼ teaspoon
pepper; pour over casserole. Cover; bake at 350°
for 1 hour. Stir in beans. Toss crumbs with
butter; sprinkle atop casserole. Bake, uncovered,
35 minutes more. Serves 12.

Creamy Broccoli Casserole

2 packages frozen broccoli
2 eggs, beaten
1 cup grated cheese
½ cup mayonnaise
1 can cream of celery soup
2 tablespoons minced onion
1 tablespoon Worcestershire sauce
Ritz cracker crumbs

Cook and drain broccoli. Mix all other
ingredients and add to broccoli. Put in buttered
casserole. Cover with cracker crumbs. Bake
uncovered for 50 minutes at 350°. Serves 6 to 8.

Zucchini Casserole

2 pounds zucchini squash
2 eggs, beaten
1 medium onion, grated or chopped
1 teaspoon salt
¼ cup grated cheese
1 large potato
½ cup milk
2 tablespoons butter, melted
pepper
¼ cup soda cracker crumbs

Wash zucchini and cut into ½ inch slices. Peel
potato and cut into ½ inch cubes. Cook together
in small amount of boiling salted water for 8 to
10 minutes. Drain well. Place in buttered
casserole dish. Combine eggs, milk, onion, butter,
salt, pepper, and cheese. Pour over vegetables.
Sprinkle with crumbs. Bake uncovered at 325°
for 25 minutes or until lightly browned and set.
Makes 6 servings.

Green Bean Casserole

2 large cans French-cut beans, drained
1 can mushrooms, drained
1 small onion, diced
½ cup grated mild cheese
1 cup cream of mushroom soup
1 small package of slivered almonds (optional)

Heat French-cut beans. Add remaining
ingredients and mix. Place in a 9 x 13 inch dish
and bake at 350° for 30 minutes. Serves 6 to 8.

Ham & Potato Casserole

Cheese & Bacon Potato Bake

1 can chicken or beef broth
5 cups potatoes, peeled and thinly sliced
1 large onion, thinly sliced
6 slices bacon
3 tablespoons all-purpose flour
1 cup shredded sharp cheddar cheese

In medium sauce pan, over medium high heat, heat broth to boil; reduce heat. Add potatoes and onion, cover and simmer 5 minutes. Drain, reserving 1½ cups broth. In skillet, over medium-high heat, fry bacon until crisp. Remove and crumble bacon; pour off all except 3 tablespoons drippings. Mix in flour and gradually add reserved broth; cook over medium heat, stirring constantly, until thickened. Stir in cheese until melted. In greased 2 quart baking dish, layer ⅓ each potato-onion mixture, sauce and bacon. Repeat layers twice. Bake at 400° for 35 minutes or until done. Makes 6 servings.

Homemade Macaroni & Cheese

1½ cups elbow macaroni
3 tablespoons butter or margarine
¼ cup finely chopped onion (optional)
2 tablespoons all-purpose flour
½ teaspoon salt
dash pepper
2 cups milk
2 cups sharp American cheese
salt

Cook macaroni according to package directions; drain. In saucepan melt butter or margarine. If using onion, cook it in butter till tender but not brown. Blend in flour, ½ teaspoon salt, and pepper. Add milk all at once; cook and stir till thickened and bubbly. Add cubed cheese to sauce; stir until melted. Then stir cheese sauce into macaroni. Turn mixture into a 1½ quart casserole. Bake, uncovered, at 350° till heated through, 30 to 35 minutes. Makes 6 servings.

Carrots Supreme

2 cups cooked carrots
¾ cup liquid from carrots
1½ tablespoon margarine
1 tablespoon chopped green pepper
1 tablespoon chopped onion
1 tablespoon flour
¼ cup cream
6 tablespoons bread crumbs

Drain liquid from carrots. Fill baking dish with carrots. Cook onions and peppers in butter until soft. Add flour. Stir. Add liquid from carrots. Add cream, salt and pepper to taste. Pour mixture over carrots. Cover top with buttered crumbs and bake at 350° for 20 minutes, or until brown. Serves 6.

Sunshine Glazed Carrots

6 or 7 medium size carrots
¼ teaspoon ginger
1 tablespoon sugar
¼ cup orange juice
1 teaspoon cornstarch
2 tablespoons margarine
¼ teaspoon salt

Slice carrots crosswise (round) about 1 inch thick. Cook, covered, in boiling, salted water until just tender; drain. Combine sugar, cornstarch, salt, and ginger in small pan. Add orange juice; cook, stirring constantly, until mixture thickens and bubbles. Stir in margarine or butter. Pour over hot carrots, tossing to coat evenly. Serve hot. Serves 4 or 5.

Carrots Supreme

Green Bean au Gratin

2 tablespoons butter
2 tablespoons flour
½ teaspoon salt
⅛ teaspoon dry mustard
¾ cup milk
¼ cup grated Longhorn cheese
1 16 ounce package frozen French-cut green beans or 16 ounce can French-cut green beans
paprika
slivered almonds
Parmesan cheese
⅓ can fried onion rings

Make a white sauce with the first five ingredients; when thick, add cheese and melt. Stir in drained beans and pour into buttered 1 quart casserole. Sprinkle with Parmesan cheese, almonds, and paprika. Bake uncovered for 30 minutes at 350°. Put onion rings on top during last 5 to 10 minutes. Serves 4.

Sour Cream Green Beans

2 packages frozen French-cut green beans
2 tablespoons bacon drippings
6 slices bacon, cooked and drained
⅔ cup sour cream

Cook beans according to directions on package; drain. Stir bacon drippings into sour cream, add to beans. Add crumbled bacon and stir over low heat until hot. Serves 8.

Corn Pudding

4 tablespoons butter
½ cup flour
1½ teaspoons salt
¾ teaspoon mustard
½ teaspoon paprika
1½ cups scalded milk
1 can cream style corn
1 egg, slightly beaten
2 teaspoons Worcestershire sauce
1 cup buttered bread crumbs

In a sauce pan melt butter; add flour mixed with the dry seasonings. Add scalded milk gradually and stirring to blend. Add corn, egg, and Worcestershire sauce. Pour into a buttered casserole dish and cover with buttered bread crumbs. Bake 350° until brown. May be stored in refrigerator overnight before baking. Makes 4 to 6 servings.

Cheesy Mixed Vegetables

1 head cauliflower, cut in florets
1 pound fresh peas, shelled or frozen
3 carrots diced in small cubes
½ pound boiling onions
3 cups milk
2 teaspoons salt
4 tablespoons whole wheat pastry flour
⅔ cup sharp Cheddar cheese, shredded.

Steam all vegetables separately until half done. Remove to a baking dish. Combine remaining ingredients and pour over the vegetables. Sprinkle with paprika. Bake uncovered at 350° until tender and brown around the edges. Yields 8 servings.

Lemon Butter

¼ cup butter
1 tablespoon fresh lemon juice
½ teaspoon salt dash cayenne
1 tablespoon finely chopped parsley

Melt butter. Add remaining ingredients. Heat and serve over cooked, hot vegetables. Makes 4 servings.

Zucchini and Tomatoes

6 medium size tomatoes, chopped
½ teaspoon oregano
6 medium size zucchini, sliced
2 tablespoons butter
1 large onion, minced
salt and pepper to taste

Melt butter in small saucepan, add vegetables and seasoning. Cook until vegetables are tender, about 10 minutes over low heat. Sprinkle with cheese if desired. Serves 4.

Herb Butter

½ cup butter
1 clove garlic, minced
¼ teaspoon oregano
¼ teaspoon
salt
freshly ground pepper
¼ cup fresh lemon juice

Melt butter in small saucepan. Add garlic and seasonings. Stir in lemon juice. Heat and pour over hot cooked vegetables. Makes 6 servings.

Old Settlers Squash in a Skillet

2 tablespoons butter or margarine
1 small onion, sliced
¼ cup water or tomato juice
2 tablespoons chopped green pepper
¼ teaspoon pepper
1 bay leaf
½ teaspoon crushed basil
2 yellow summer squash
2 medium zucchini
salt to taste

Melt butter in skillet. Saute onion slightly. Add liquid and green pepper. Cover and cook 5 minutes. Add pepper, bay leaf, basil and squash. Cover and simmer until squash is tender. Do not overcook. Salt to taste. Serves 6.

Stuffed Acorn Squash

2 acorn squash cut in half, remove seeds and fibers
cinnamon
4 teaspoons brown sugar
1 cup unsweetened apple sauce
4 teaspoons soft margarine

Place squash halves, cut side down, in shallow baking pan. Cover bottom with water. Bake at 400° for 50 to 60 minutes or until tender. Turn squash over. Fill each cavity with applesauce and brown sugar. Dot with margarine. Sprinkle with cinnamon. Continue baking until applesauce is bubbly, about 15 minutes. Makes 4 servings.

Potatoes au Gratin

4 cups peeled, boiled potatoes, finely diced
1 cup Cheddar cheese, shredded
2 tablespoons onion, finely chopped
2 tablespoons butter
1 cup milk
2 eggs
2 teaspoons salt
freshly grated pepper
½ cup cheese, shredded

Arrange alternate layers of potatoes and cheese in buttered 1½ quart baking dish. Sprinkle each layer with onion; dot with butter. Mix eggs, milk and seasonings. Pour over potato mixture. Sprinkle with additional shredded cheese. Bake for 45 minutes at 350°. Serves 6.

Scalloped Cabbage with Cheese

1 small head cabbage (1½ pound)
1 cup medium white sauce
½ cup grated cheese
buttered bread crumbs
1 cup soft bread cubed or ¾ cup dry bread crumbs
1 tablespoon butter

Cut cabbage in several large pieces. Discard stem. Cover cabbage in boiling salted water for 5 to 7 minutes. Drain liquid. Layer in greased baking dish—cabbage, cheese and white sauce. Mix bread crumbs and butter in separate pan. Place over cabbage mixture. Bake in 400° oven until bread crumbs are browned. Serves 6.

Yummy Yams and Apples

6 to 8 yams; cook until tender; slice
6 to 8 medium apples, sliced
Layer apples and yams. End with apples on top.
Sauce:
1 cup sugar
½ teaspoon salt
4 tablespoons cornstarch
¼ pound butter

Bring to boil 2 cups of water. Slowly pour over mixed dry ingredients, stir to blend. Cook until thick. Pour over apples and yams. Bake at 375° for 45 minutes. Yields 12 servings.

Cheese-Fried Zucchini

¼ cup cracker crumbs
2 tablespoons grated Parmesan cheese
2 tablespoons flour
1 tablespoon salt
2 zucchini, thinly sliced
1 egg beaten
2 to 4 tablespoons oil

In plastic bag or shallow bowl, combine bread crumbs, cheese, flour and salt. Dip zucchini in egg, then coat with crumb mixture. Fry in hot oil in skillet till golden brown and crispy, turning occasionally. Serves 3 to 4.

Cauliflower with Mushrooms

1 medium head cauliflower, broken into florets
½ pound fresh mushrooms, washed, or 1 can whole mushrooms
White Sauce:
⅓ cup butter
¼ cup flour
1 teaspoon salt
2 cups milk
6 slices pimento cheese

Parboil the cauliflower and put into a casserole dish. Melt butter in saucepan over low heat. Blend flour and salt. Add milk all at once, stirring constantly until mixture thickens and bubbles. Add pimento cheese and mushrooms to the sauce. Pour sauce over cauliflower in casserole dish. Cover and place in oven at 350° until cauliflower is finished cooking, 10 to 15 minutes. Serves 4 to 6.

Bottled Apple Pie Filling

4½ cups sugar
1 cup cornstarch
2 teaspoons cinnamon
¼ to ½ teaspoon nutmeg
1 teaspoon salt
10 cups water
3 tablespoons lemon juice
2 or 3 drops of yellow food coloring
3 teaspoons dehydrated lemon peel (optional)
apples, peeled and sliced, about 6 pounds

Blend the first five ingredients together. Then stir in water. Cook and stir until thick. Then add lemon juice, yellow food coloring and dehydrated lemon peel. Fold apples into cooked mixture. Heat thoroughly. Pack into sterilized hot quart jars, leaving 1 inch of head space. Put into hot water bath and process for 20 minutes. One quart makes a 9 inch pie.

Apple Butter

8 pounds apples
5½ cups sugar
1½ tablespoons ground cloves
2 cups water
1 tablespoon ground cinnamon
1 teaspoon ground allspice

Wash the apples. Do not peel or core. Remove stems and quarter the apples. Place in a kettle, add water and cover. Cook the apples until apples are soft. Rub apples through a sieve. Combine with sugar and spices. There should be about 10 cups of apple pulp.

" . . . Every fruit in the season thereof; to be used with prudence and thanksgiving." (Doctrine and Covenants, Section 89, Verse 11). The Mormons are a resourceful people. They are counseled by their leaders to plant gardens and take advantage of fruits and vegetables during their seasons of plenty. Canning is used to preserve the fruits and vegetables for use during the entire year. Many Mormon families prepare themselves for times of hardship by setting aside a year supply of food.

Bread and Butter Pickles

4 quarts cucumbers, sliced, unpeeled
5 large onions, sliced thick
4 red or green peppers, sliced
2 cups sugar
2 teaspoons turmeric
2 cups vinegar
1 teaspoon dry mustard
4 teaspoons celery seeds
4 teaspoons mustard seeds

Sprinkle cucumbers, onions, and green peppers with hand full of salt. Cover with water, stand overnight in enamel kettle. Drain off liquid and add sugar, turmeric, vinegar, dry mustard, celery seeds, and mustard seeds. Mix all up and pour over mixture. Let boil 5 minutes before bottling. Makes 8 to 10 pints.

Pickled Beets

10 pounds raw fresh beets (medium size with tops and tails). Adjust amount used to individual needs
1 quart vinegar
½ cup sugar
1 teaspoon salt
Choice of:
½ teaspoon ginger
1 teaspoon cinnamon or
1 teaspoon whole cloves

Wash beets in cold water. Leave tails on and cut steams and leaves off no shorter than 3 inches from beet. Place in large enamel pan, cover with water and bring to boil over high heat. Note: depending on the size of cooker available, more than one batch may be required to cook the beets. Cook until beets are tender. Remove from heat, allow to cool; slip skins and stems and discard; place cooked beets in clean, sterilized pint or quart jars. Note: slice, quarter, or leave beets whole, depending on preference. Combine above ingredients in heavy sauce pan. Bring to boil and cook one minute. Remove from heat and cool. Pour mixture over bottled beets, seal with lids and rings, and place on rack in cold packing kettle with lid. Add enough water to container to cover jars. Place on stove on high heat and gradually bring to boil; let beets boil for 10 minutes. Turn heat off and let processed beets stand in water until cool enough to remove bottles safely. Tighten lids and allow jars to set over night until sealed. Makes 20 pints.

Chokecherry Jelly

To prepare fruit:
Wash berries. It is not necessary to remove stems from fruit. To 1 gallon of berries, add 10 cups water, bring to boil, and boil for 15 minutes. Drain juice off through colander or strainer. Add 10 more cups water, mash berries well, and boil for 5 to 10 minutes. Press through colander, working through all pulp possible, but not seeds or skins.

To make jelly:
5 cups chokecherry juice
2 ounce package powdered pectin
7 cups sugar

Place chokecherry juice in a large kettle, add the powdered pectin, and bring to boil. Add sugar. Bring to boil again and cook for 5 minutes. Remove from heat, pour into hot sterilized jelly glasses, and seal with hot paraffin wax.
Note: By substituting 1 cup unsweetened apple juice for 1 cup berry juice jelly will be more firm. Makes 6 pints.

Strawberry-Peach Jam

5 cups peeled crushed peaches
½ cup lemon juice
1 16 ounce package frozen strawberries
1½ packages powdered pectin
3½ cups sugar
red food coloring

Combine crushed peaches, lemon juice, and frozen strawberries, bring to a good boil. Add sugar and red food coloring to individual preference. Bring to another good boil that cannot be stirred down, then boil for 4 minutes. Remove from heat, pour into hot sterilized pint jars and seal. Makes 6 pints.
This jam is quite thin; if you desire, add 2 packages pectin. The fruit floats to the top when jam cools. When you open a jar to serve, stir it up.

Deep-Dish Apple Pie

12 medium tart apples
½ teaspoon ground cinnamon
¼ teaspoon ground nutmeg
3 tablespoons butter or margarine
⅓ cup shortening
all-purpose flour
salt
cold milk
sugar
light cream

Peel, core and thinly slice apples; place in large bowl. Mix 1 cup sugar, 3 tablespoons flour, cinnamon, nutmeg, and ¼ teaspoon salt; sprinkle over apples. Mix well. Turn into 12 x 7½ x 2 inch baking dish; dot with butter. Stir 1 cup flour with ⅛ teaspoon salt; cut in shortening till crumbly. Gradually add 2 to 3 teaspoons milk, toss with fork to just dampen. Form into a ball. On lightly floured surface, roll to 13 X 8½ inch rectangle. Place over apples; flute edges. Brush with milk; cut slits for escape of steam. Sprinkle with sugar. Bake at 400° for 40 to 45 minutes. Serve warm with cream. Makes 8 servings.

Pumpkin Pie

1 cup sugar
½ teaspoon ginger
1½ teaspoons cinnamon
½ teaspoon salt
½ teaspoon cloves
½ teaspoon allspice
1½ cups canned pumpkin*
2 eggs
1⅔ cup evaporated milk (1 large can)
½ teaspoon nutmeg
1 9 inch single-crust unbaked pie shell

Blend sugar, spices and salt together. Add pumpkin. Mix well. Beat eggs with milk and combine with pumpkin mixture until smooth. Pour filling into unbaked pie shell. Bake in hot oven at 425° for 15 minutes. Reduce heat to 350° and continue baking 35 minutes, or until knife inserted in pie comes out clean. Cool before slicing. Serves 8.
*If desired, cooked, mashed sweet potatoes or squash may be used in place of pumpkin.

Rhubarb and Cherry Pie

1 pound rhubarb, cut in ½ inch slices (4 cups)
1 16 ounce can pitted tart red cherries, drained
1½ cups sugar
¼ cup quick-cooking tapioca
3 drops red food coloring
pastry for 9 inch lattice-top pie

Combine fruits, sugar, tapioca and food coloring; let stand 15 minutes. Line 9 inch pie plate with pastry; pour in filling. Adjust lattice top; seal and flute edges. Bake at 400° for 40 to 50 minutes; cover pastry edges with foil to avoid overbrowning, if needed. Cut in 8 pieces.

No-Fail Pie Crust

2½ cups sifted flour
1 cup shortening
¼ cup cold water
1 tablespoon vinegar
1 teaspoon salt
1 large egg, beaten

Sift together flour and salt, cut in shortening until mixture resembles small peas. In a mixing bowl combine water, vinegar and egg. Pour into flour mixture and mix lightly until all flour is moistened and pastry forms a ball. Divide dough as desired, roll out on flour board; line 9 inch pie plate, and fill with favorite filling or bake as pastry shell for 10 minutes at 450°. Makes 3 single crusts.

Pioneer Bread Pudding

1 cup flour
1 cup sugar
2 cups bread crumbs
1 teaspoon nutmeg
¼ cup butter, melted
1 cup milk

Mix flour, sugar, and crumbs, add nutmeg, mix thoroughly. Add butter and milk. Steam in double boiler for 1 hour. Serve hot with sauce.
Sauce:
3 tablespoons butter
1 cup sugar
3 cups hot water
½ cup flour

Add butter and sugar to hot water. Bring to a boil. Add flour made into a soft paste. Add to hot syrup and stir well. Boil 1 minute.

Mom's Apple Pudding

Cream together:
1 cup sugar
¼ cup shortening
1 egg
3 large apples, grated
1 cup flour
1 teaspoon baking soda
½ teaspoon salt
½ teaspoon nutmeg
½ cup nuts

Cream together sugar and shortening. Mix in the egg and grated apples. Then add the remaining ingredients. Mix well. Spread in 9 x 13 inch cake pan which has been greased. Bake for 30 to 40 minutes at 350°. Serve warm with caramel sauce.

Caramel Sauce
1 square butter
2 cups brown sugar
2 cups boiling water
3 rounded tablespoons flour made into a paste

Melt butter and brown sugar together in pan over low heat. Cook several minutes until it is caramelize. Avoid burning. Add the boiling water and flour paste. Cook several minutes to thicken.

Canned Fruit Cobbler

½ cup sugar
1 tablespoon cornstarch
2½ canned fruit juice (cherries, peaches, berries)
cinnamon
1 cup flour
1 tablespoon sugar
1½ teaspoons baking powder
½ teaspoon salt
3 tablespoons shortening
½ cup milk

Preheat oven to 400°. In saucepan, mix sugar and cornstarch. Stir fruit and juice in gradually. Bring to boil for 1 minute, stirring constantly. Pour into 1½ quart baking dish, dot with butter and sprinkle witn cinnamon.
Sift together flour, sugar, baking powder and salt. Cut in shortening until crumbly and stir in the milk. Drop by the spoonsfuls onto hot fruit in baking dish. Bake until golden brown, serve with cream.

Old Fashioned Oatmeal Cookies

1 cup raisins
1 cup water
¾ cup shortening
1½ cups sugar
2 eggs
1 teaspoon vanilla
2½ cups flour
1 teaspoon soda
1 teaspoon salt
1 teaspoon cinnamon
½ teaspoon baking powder
½ teaspoon cloves
2 cups rolled oats
½ cup chopped nuts

Simmer raisins and water over medium heat until raisins are plump, about 15 minutes. Drain raisins, reserving the liquid. Add enough water to reserved liquid to measure ½ cup. Mix thoroughly shortening, sugar, eggs and vanilla. Stir in reserved liquid. Blend in remaining ingredients. Drop dough by rounded teaspoonful about 2 inches apart onto ungreased baking sheet. Bake at 400° for 8 to 10 minutes, until light brown. Yield about 6½ dozen.

Tangy Lemon Bars

2 cups flour
1 cup butter or margarine
½ cup powdered sugar
½ teaspoon salt

Cream these 4 ingredients and press into a 9 x 13 inch pan and bake 15 minutes at 350°.

Topping:
1¾ cup sugar
4 eggs, beaten
½ teaspoon baking powder
4 tablespoons flour
juice and rind of 1 lemon

Blend together in blender. Pour this over hot crust and bake for 30 minutes at 350°. Remove from oven and sprinkle with powdered sugar. Makes 15 to 20 bars.

Nutty Apple Cake

2 eggs
1 cup salad oil
2 cups sugar
2 cups flour
2 teaspoons cinnamon
1 teaspoon soda
½ teaspoon salt
1 teaspoon vanilla
4 cups peeled thinly sliced apples
½ cup chopped nuts

Beat eggs until foamy. Add oil and sugar and stir. Add sifted dry ingredients. Add apples and nuts, just folding them in, do not stir hard. Bake in 9x13 inch pan at 350° for 60 minutes. Cool and ice.

Icing:
6 ounces cream cheese
1½ cups powdered sugar
3 tablespoons butter
1 teaspoon vanilla
milk

Beat cream cheese until soft. Add remaining ingredients and milk as needed. Beat until light and fluffy. Yields 15 to 20 servings.

Grandma's Spice Cake

2 cups sifted flour
½ teaspoon soda
2 teaspoons baking powder
½ teaspoon salt
½ teaspoon nutmeg
1 teaspoon cinnamon
¼ teaspoon cloves
½ cup shortening
1 cup sugar
2 eggs
1 cup buttermilk or sour milk

Sift dry ingredients together twice. Cream shortening and add sugar. Beat in eggs one-at-a-time. Add buttermilk to creamed mixture alternately with dry ingredients. May be baked in layer pans or in a 8x12 inch pan for 30 minutes at 350 to 375°. Cupcakes may be made from this recipe. One cup raisins and ½ cup chopped nuts may be added. Add these to the dry ingredients for easier mixing. Serves 16 to 20.

Grandma's Spice Cake

Dad's Divinity

2½ cups sugar
½ cup light corn syrup
1½ cups water
¼ teaspoon salt
2 egg whites
½ teaspoons vanilla
½ cup chopped walnuts

Butter sides of a heavy 2 quart saucepan. In it combine sugar, corn syrup, water, and salt. Cook to 260°, stirring only until sugar dissolves. Meanwhile, as temperature of syrup reaches 250°, beat egg whites in small mixer bowl until stiff peaks form, but not dry. Add the syrup gradually to the egg whites, beating at high speed on electric mixer. Add vanilla and beat until candy holds its shape, about five minutes. Candy will just start to lose its gloss. Quickly stir in nuts and spread into a lightly buttered 8 inch square pan. Cool before cutting into 36 pieces. Divinity may also be dropped in peaked teaspoonfuls onto waxed paper.

Caramel Corn

2 cubes butter or margarine
2 cups brown sugar
½ cup white corn syrup
Boil 5 minutes. Remove from heat and add:
½ teaspoon soda
1 teaspoon vanilla
2 gallons popped corn

Cover popped corn with syrup. Bake on cookie sheet in 250° oven for 1 hour. Stir every 15 minutes.

Puffed Rice Balls

4 quarts puffed rice
½ cup light corn syrup
2 cups sugar
1 cup water
1 teaspoon salt
1 tablespoon butter
1 teaspoon vanilla

Cook to soft crack stage, 243°. Pour over puffed rice. Shape into balls.

Old Fashioned Vanilla and Berry Ice Cream

Vanilla ice cream:
2 cups milk
1 cup sugar
1 tablespoon flour
¼ teaspoon salt
3 egg yolks, slightly beaten
3 cups cream
2 teaspoons vanilla extract

Variations:
Follow directions for vanilla ice cream. Just before freezing, blend in 2 cups crushed strawberries or raspberries.

Scald milk in double boiler over simmering water. Combine sugar, flour, and salt; mix well. Add gradually to milk, stirring constantly, and cook over direct heat 5 minutes. Remove from heat and vigorously stir about 3 tablespoons of hot mixture into egg yolks. Immediately stir into hot mixture in top of double boiler. Return to heat and cook over simmering water 10 minutes, stirring constantly until mixture coats a metal spoon. Remove from heat and cool. Stir in cream and vanilla extract. Chill in refrigerator.

For Dasher-type Freezer: Fill chilled container two-thirds full with ice cream mixture. Cover tightly. Set into freezer tub and, alternating layers, fill with 8 parts crushed ice and 1 part rock salt. Turn handle slowly 5 minutes. Turn rapidly until handle becomes very difficult to turn (about 15 minutes). Remove dasher. Pack down ice cream and cover with waxed paper. Put lid on top again and fill opening for dasher with cork. Repack freezer in ice using 4 parts ice and 1 part rock salt. Cover with heavy paper or cloth. Let ripen 2 to 3 hours.

For refrigerator: Pour the chilled mixture into refrigerator trays and place in freezer compartment of refrigerator. When mixture becomes mush, turn into chilled bowl and beat with chilled rotary beater. This helps to form fine crystals and give a smooth creamy mixture. Return mixture to trays and freeze until firm. Makes about 1½ quarts ice cream.